MORE TO
LIFE

ENGAGING THROUGH STORY

DENNIS PETHERS

LifeWay Press®
Nashville, Tennessee

ISBN 978-1-4158-7369-4
Item 005502440

Dewey decimal classification: 269.2
Subject heading: EVANGELISTIC WORK

To order additional copies of this resource: write to LifeWay Church Resources Customer Service; One LifeWay Plaza; Nashville, TN 37234-0113; fax (615) 251-5933; phone toll free (800) 458-2772; order online at www.lifeway.com; e-mail orderentry@lifeway.com; or visit the LifeWay Christian Store serving you.

Printed in the United States of America

Leadership and Adult Publishing
LifeWay Church Resources
One LifeWay Plaza
Nashville, TN 37234-0175

Contents

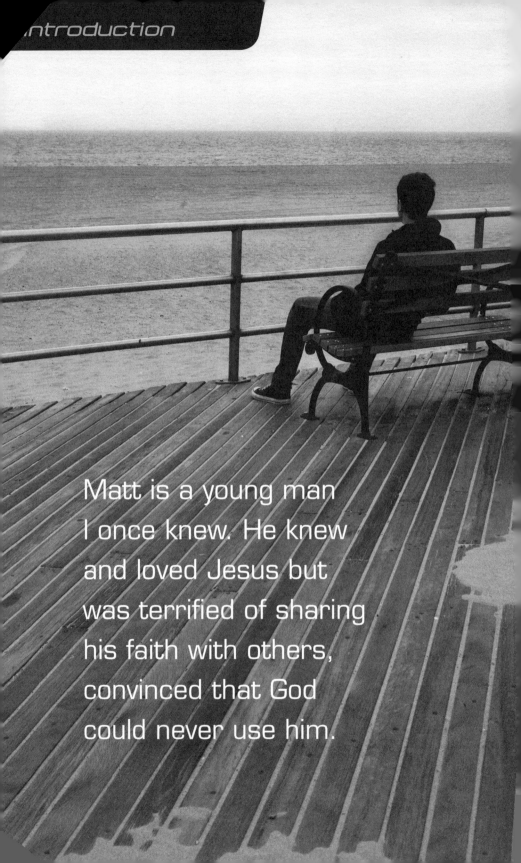

Matt is a young man
I once knew. He knew
and loved Jesus but
was terrified of sharing
his faith with others,
convinced that God
could never use him.

I can still see the joy on Matt's face as he rushed toward me at a coffee bar calling out aloud, wearing a grin that seemed to consume his entire face. "I did it! I did it," he called at the top of his voice. "I told him about how God changed my life, and he wanted God to change his. I can't believe it. It's brilliant!"

Because of Matt's witness a young man gave his life to Christ. He was utterly transformed—and so was Matt. The young man was transformed into a believer, and Matt was transformed into a believer who believed that God could use him to win a lost person. He was never the same again!

Wouldn't it be great if God could do that in your life? He can!

God's Heart
Participating in *More to Life: Engaging Through Story* will help you to see and believe that God can use you. It begins by a key emphasis that evangelism—telling others the good news—is not something that we do as a chore or to recruit more people to our church. It is essentially something that we do because it is an expression of the heart of God Himself. He loves the lost and sent Jesus to seek and to save them. As we open our hearts to Him, we begin to see lost people as He sees them.

My Part
As we begin to discover and feel God's heart, then we can each play our part. You will discover that this does not require that you become a great preacher or brilliant theologian. Your part is probably best summed up as sharing what you are experiencing of God with people who don't know Him.

Whoever you are and whatever you are like, God can and will use you to reach out to others and help them to discover the good news. This is what Matt experienced, and you can too!

Video sessions are available for download at *www.lifeway.com/downloads*.

SESSION ONE

Causing Heaven
to Rejoice

"I tell you, in the same way, there will be more joy in heaven over one sinner who repents than over 99 righteous people who don't need repentance."

LUKE 15:7

Joy is perhaps the emotion that we crave most and experience least, often momentary and yet always memorable. In Luke 15, Jesus speaks to a crowd, made up of those who thought they were righteous and those who were known as sinners, to explain an amazing truth—God the Father is filled with joy when sinners repent!

Jesus speaks of a shepherd searching for a lost sheep, a woman searching for a lost coin, and two sons who have lost their way with their father. Joy comes when the lost are found and redemption comes to the rebellious. As Luke 15:7 shows, for all of the things which could bring joy in heaven, a sinner's spiritual transformation stands out as one of the greatest causes for celebration.

The teaching from Christ in Luke 15 begs for a question to be asked: What causes joy on earth? Specifically, what causes joy on the piece of earth where you and I live?

INTRODUCTION (5 minutes)

Leader: Use the "Introduction" material to begin today's session.

To be like God, we should rejoice for the same thing—a lost person coming to know God. When a person turns their life from a "me-centered" life toward a "God-centered" life, our joy should be uncontrollable. In this week's session, we will take a close look at our hearts and rediscover a great passion for sharing the gospel with lost people—those who Jesus came to seek and to save.

Evangelism, telling others about Jesus, should be done out of joy. It is not a duty we should perform out of guilt. It begins by grasping God's compassion for the lost and gaining His desire to reach them.

During *More to Life: Engaging Through Story* we will not aim to add to any feelings of failure or guilt that you may have. Rather, we want you to see the things God longs to do in and through every one of us.

> Leader: Guide participants through a time of introducing themselves to one another.

OPENING SHARE TIME
(8 minutes)

Getting to Know You
A key aspect in gaining confidence and desire to share our faith is by becoming comfortable about discussing it with friends. Talking about our lives and discovering how God is working in others can be motivational and encouraging.

Break into groups of two or three and share some information about your life. Some of the things you share may include:
- Where you live; family; work; leisure interests
- What has been the most fun, exciting, or memorable thing you have ever done?
- What is the thing that you admire most about Jesus?

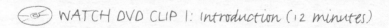 WATCH DVD CLIP 1: Introduction (12 minutes)

> Leader: Guide participants through the following questions.

Dennis had a fascinating encounter in the carpet store.

- Do you know someone who was surprised to discover that Christians are "normal people" instead of "religious people"?

- How should we react to unbelievers who show this surprise?

Key Question

What is the most difficult: To get people outside of church interested in Jesus or to get people inside of church interested enough in people outside of church to tell them about Jesus?

In groups of three or four, discuss the Key Question by answering the following questions:
- Which do you think is most difficult?
- What makes each of them difficult?
- What might help believers become more interested in people outside of church?
- Do you ever feel guilty for not being very good at sharing Jesus with others? How do you handle these feelings?

Leader: Following the discussion time spend some time discussing each group's answers.

GROUP DISCUSSION (5 minutes)

- What would encourage you to want to tell other people about Jesus? Do we view them as God views them? Why or why not? Be honest as you discuss your passion for the lost as it compares with God's passion. There is no condemnation, no need for us to feel guilty—God can change us!

Jesus' declaration in Luke 19:10, "The Son of Man has come to seek and to save the lost," is the climax of a section of the gospel that begins in Luke 15. At the center of Jesus' words and actions is His sharing in the Father's passion for lost people. This is how He wants His followers to be, not self-interested. Those who love God will share His passion for the lost.

- How do you feel when you consider the picture that Jesus paints of the loving Father who is filled with joy when the lost son returns? How do you react to the description of God from the DVD as being "absolutely passionate"?

The Passionometer is a rough "measure" of the depth of our passion for telling others about Jesus. It can help us to be honest about where we really are in relation to sharing our faith.

- What do you expect would be the result if we tested the passion of our church to sharing faith? Would our church be passionate or apathetic? What leads you to this conclusion?

Leader: Guide participants through the following questions and spend time teaching about the Passionometer.

ACTIVITY
The Passionometer (10 minutes)

Do we attend church without a thought to the lost, or do we see every day as an opportunity to help others come to a better understanding of Jesus? The Passionometer is a simple measure of your desire to reach the lost around you and increase your passion.

Directions:
Each person should honestly place a circle around the number that represents where they think they are on the scale. Ask them to share it with the person next to them or with a close friend in the group. Share what they have circled and pray with one another that God's passion will grow in them.

PASSIONOMETER			
1 2 3	Never witnessed to anyone and have no desire	Need a change of heart	Self interested
4 5 6 7	Would like to witness more but hesitant	Need encouragement and equipping	Feel guilty
8 9 10	Always witnessing	Totally committed to God's passion for the lost	Motivated

Each of us will have been challenged in different ways during this session regarding our passion for evangelism and the lost.

- What are some of the common excuses believers give for not sharing their faith? What are the major obstacles you face to sharing your faith in Christ?

- How can passion help you in overcoming common obstacles to talking to others about Jesus?

- What causes the greatest joy in your church? In your life?

 WATCH DVD CLIP 2:
Sharing in God's Passion (4 minutes)

- What is your reaction to Dennis's story of the man who was asked to leave church because he was dressed poorly?

- Dennis said, "If God loves the lost, then we will love the lost too, if we love God." How do you react to this statement?

- What are the temptations we face as believers to act more as the older brother in the parable found in Luke 15:11-31?

- God can change us and, through us, change the world. What changes are needed in our lives to love the lost?

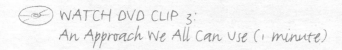 WATCH DVD CLIP 3:
An Approach We All Can Use (1 minute)

GROUP DISCUSSION (5 minutes)

- Discuss Dennis' definition for evangelism:
  "Evangelism is leaving the person that I've met with a better understanding of God than they would have had if they had never met me."

- Review the parts of the four-story approach to sharing your faith in Christ. How do you react to a method of sharing your faith that is as simple as telling your story?

- How do you feel about trusting God to use you to witness to others?

SUMMARY AND PRAYER
(5 minutes)

Leader: Give an overview of the Personal Engagement section of the workbook.

Everyone is encouraged to do the Personal Engagement section of their books. This can be done in one sitting but it is probably best to do this over several days in order to give time for reflection.

Each week, the Personal Engagement section will include:
- Bible Encounter—getting to grips with Scripture that is relevant to what is being discovered and experienced.
- Reflection—personalizing what is being experienced and responding to God.
- Stepping Out—practical things we can do outside of our comfort zone.
- Prayer—transparently opening ourselves up to God.
- Building Each Other Up—noting things that we are experiencing that may be good to share with others during the group discussions.

Prayer Time
Through prayer, we can come to know and reflect God's heart for the unbelievers around us. Perhaps some in the group need to become passionate about the lost whereas others need to begin acting on their passion.

Prayer Emphasis
Pray for one another, that God will fill each one with a passion and confidence to share their story with one person.

Video sessions are available for download at *www.lifeway.com/downloads*.

Personal Engagement

Personal activities you can do throughout the week that will help you to remain focused on the lessons and discussions from the session.

BIBLE ENCOUNTER

Read Ezekiel 34:1-31 and answer the following questions:

- What is God's major complaint against the religious leaders in verses 2-4?

- How is this complaint amplified in verses 18-19?

- How will God deal with the religious leaders (vv. 7-10)?

- What will God do to ensure the lost sheep are cared for (vv. 11-16; 22-24; 30-31)?

- What does this story have to say about the way that Christians should view the lost?

Read Luke 18:9-14 and consider the following questions:

- In what ways do you see yourself in both of the characters in this parable?

The Pharisee:

The Tax Collector:

- How would you like to be changed?

Read Matthew 9:35-38 and consider the following questions:

- What caused Jesus to have compassion on the crowds?

- What did He tell His disciples to do?

- What is the key way this prayer will be answered in Luke 10:2-3?

- How does this passage affect how you view your community?

REFLECTION

God's plan for our salvation is a story filled with passion. The apostle Paul writes in Romans 5:8:

> "God proves His own love for us in that while we were still sinners, Christ died for us!"

If ever there was an example of compassion—here it is! Look at the following examples from the Gospels of Matthew and Mark then use the space to write down the things that most impact you about knowing what Jesus experienced so that we, sinners, could come to know God.

You may find it helpful to find a quiet place and read these verses aloud to yourself. Speaking the Scripture aloud gives it an extra reinforcement in our lives. Frequently pause—just to take it in!

Matthew 27:27-31

"The governor's soldiers took Jesus into headquarters and gathered the whole company around Him. They stripped Him and dressed Him in a scarlet military robe. They twisted together a crown of thorns, put it on His head, and placed a reed in His right hand. And they knelt down before Him and mocked Him: "Hail, King of the Jews!" Then they spit on Him, took the reed, and kept hitting Him on the head. When they had mocked Him, they stripped Him of the robe, put His clothes on Him, and led Him away to crucify Him."

Mark 15:25-32

"It was nine in the morning when they crucified Him. The inscription of the charge written against Him was: THE KING OF THE JEWS.

"They crucified two criminals with Him, one on His right and one on His left. So the Scripture was fulfilled that says: 'And He was counted among outlaws.' Those who passed by were yelling insults at Him, shaking their heads, and saying, 'Ha! The One who would demolish the sanctuary and build it in three days, save Yourself by coming down from the cross!' In the same way, the chief priests with the scribes were mocking Him to one another and saying, 'He saved others; He cannot save Himself! Let the Messiah, the King of Israel, come down now from the cross, so that we may see and believe.' Even those who were crucified with Him were taunting Him."

Matthew 27:45-47

"From noon until three in the afternoon darkness came over the whole land. About three in the afternoon Jesus cried out with a loud voice, 'Elí, Elí, lemá sabachtháni?' that is, 'My God, My God, why have You forsaken Me?'

"When some of those standing there heard this, they said, 'He's calling for Elijah!' "

From these three passages, what lessons do you see that affect how you share your faith? Write down how your passion should develop for those around you in the space below.

STEPPING OUT

Everyday, you are surrounded by people who are lost. As you see and meet lost people this week, ask God to help you to see them as He sees them. As this begins to happen, use the space below to note ways and circumstances in which you have sensed or are sensing God's prompting, what is happening, and how it is changing how you feel about God, yourself, and the lost people around you.

WHO DO YOU KNOW?

In the diagram below, each circle represents a "world" in which you live. Within each world there are people you connect with on different levels. Take time to write in the names of people that "live" in these worlds.

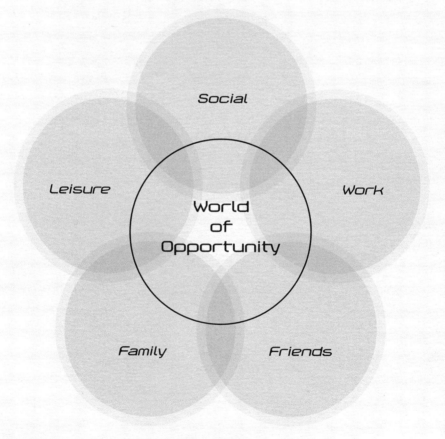

Social

Leisure

Work

World of Opportunity

Family

Friends

Once completed, consider three names from all of those you have written in the circles. These names represent three people that you feel you have the best opportunity to "help have a better understanding of God because they have met you." Write these names in the center circle, which represents your "World of Opportunity." Begin praying for these people by name, asking God to make them curious about Jesus. Pray for God to make you aware of opportunities to share your faith with them.

PRAYER

God wants us to share His immense passion for the lost. If we lack this passion, ask to share in His. God wants you to have it! Take some time to write a personal letter to God about how you feel and ask Him to help you to change.

Dear God,

Once you have written your letter, read it aloud as a prayer to God.

BUILDING EACH OTHER UP

As you have spent time during this week engaging in all sorts of things that have challenged you, it may be that there are things that you have learned or experienced that you feel it would be good to share with the other members of the group. These may be things that will really encourage them or things that you would like to share because you feel you need help, advice, or encouragement.

Use the space below to make a note of these things so that you don't forget what you wanted to share!

Discovering the "Far from God" People Around You

"You will receive power when the Holy Spirit has come on you, and you will be My witnesses in Jerusalem, in all Judea and Samaria, and to the ends of the earth."
Acts 1:8

When you look out the front window of your home, what do you see? Can you picture it in your mind right now? It might be a tree, a street lamp, another home across the street, or an adjacent building. Most likely, you can picture it in your mind. But here's another question: When you look up from the normal activity of your daily life, who is usually there?

Every day, we are surrounded by people. Spouses, children, friends, coworkers, and anonymous people pass through our field of vision constantly. As Christians, our primary concern for each one should be to see them as God sees them. Tragically, we are surrounded by "far from God" people daily. This week, we will begin learning to gauge people's receptivity to the message of Jesus and how our own relationship with Him can be used as a powerful tool in God's hands.

INTRODUCTION (5 minutes)

Leader: Use the "Introduction" material to begin today's session.

In the previous session we looked at God's passion for lost people. This helped us to see our need to share in His passion and have a desire for lost people to come to know Jesus. It relates to the difficulty on those inside the church becoming interested enough in people outside the church to tell them about Jesus. In this session, we will think and talk about those outside the church—the people that God is passionate for us to reach. What are they like, and how will we encourage their desire to find out more about Jesus?

OPENING SHARE TIME
(5 minutes)

> Leader: Lead participants through a review of last week's session and Personal Engagement.

Take a few minutes to share what you recorded in your "Building Each Other Up" space.

- What specific actions do you need to take to be more passionate about witnessing?

- What effect did the biblical passages have on your passions?

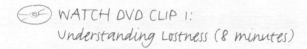 WATCH DVD CLIP 1:
    Understanding Lostness (8 minutes)

> Leader: Guide participants to complete the activities and answer the following questions.

ACTIVITY
The Graspometer (10 minutes)

The Graspometer is a rough "measure" that helps us see at-a-glance where people are in their understanding of the truth about Jesus. Lost people are becoming increasingly farther away from an understanding of God and less aware of His love for them. Using the Graspometer, write in the names of five people that you know in the appropriate place on the scale. These may be five of the names that you wrote down during your Personal Engagement time during the past week. If a friend named Paul has very little understanding of anything to do with Jesus you would write his name around the number -9.

Our challenge is how to reach people not at the top of the scale!

GRASPOMETER			
0	Full grasp of the Christian faith	Most evangelistic activity	Churched
-1			
-2			
-3			
-4			
-5	Belief in God but not committed	People becoming increasingly lost. This is where witness must be increased.	Less churched
-6			
-7			
-8			
-9			
-10	No idea that God exists	Often totally unreached	Never churched

As you look at the Graspometer and consider the understanding of God that people "close to you" have, discuss the following:

- How do you react to the story Dennis told about the boy in church who asked regarding Jesus, "Who's that on the wall?" What people do you know who may have said something similar about Jesus?

- It has been said, "When people stop believing in God they don't believe in nothing, they believe in anything." Does this quote describe people you know? Who?

- People are getting farther and farther from God but they are close to us. How could the changes they see in our lives help them to "climb" the Graspometer so that we are reaching people who are farther away than -1?

- How would you explain your faith in a way that people who are far from God would understand it? How would you explain words that are familiar to Christians to people that have never heard them?

	We mean	An unbeliever may think
Saved		
Lost		
Sin		
Salvation		
Redeemed		
Washed in the blood		

GROUP DISCUSSION *(5 minutes)*

The way *More to Life* defines evangelism is helpful in demonstrating how every believer can play their part in helping lost people better understand Jesus or climb higher on the Graspometer.

Review the *More to Life* definition of evangelism:
"Leaving the person I have met with a better understanding of God than they would have had if they had never met me."

- How does this definition help us to reach people who are slipping away from an understanding of God as demonstrated by the Graspometer? Discuss what role simple conversation can have in helping the unbelievers in a circle of friends and influence begin to better grasp the life of Jesus.

ACTIVITY
World of Opportunity (8 minutes)

During your Personal Engagement time there was an opportunity to complete a diagram "Who Do You Know?" (p. 18). Break into pairs and refer to the completed diagram. (If necessary, take some time to complete this diagram now.) Without breaking any confidences, talk to each other about the people who are in your "World of Opportunity" circle.

- How open are they to the gospel?

- Roughly, where do they fall on the Graspometer? (See p. 23.)

- Share feelings of your hopes and fears as you trust God to help you to make and take opportunities to share your faith with these people.

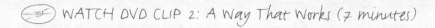 WATCH DVD CLIP 2: A Way That Works (7 minutes)

Leader: Guide participants to answer the following questions.

On the DVD, Dennis underlined the *More to Life* principle that "Changed lives authenticate the message of Jesus."

It is the story of our changed lives that is most likely to arouse interest in the mind and heart of a person who is not familiar with the Bible and church. This challenge must motivate us into taking these opportunities—we must not remain at a distance and long for things to be like they were.

- Dennis told the story of the penguin standing on the rock and only occasionally eating a fish. How does this story relate to your church?

- Is your church "on the rock" or "in the water"?

- How about you? Where do you spend the majority of your time: on the rock or in the water?

- Discuss how we see the rescuing nature of God through: Old Testament personalities such as Moses and Gideon and New Testament personalities such as Paul, Peter, and Jesus Christ.

ACTIVITY
The Four-Story Approach *(5 minutes)*

To help you grasp the evangelistic approach in *More to Life*, fill in
each box with the proper story:

Story 1

Story 2

Story 3

Story 4

Answers: 1—Their Stories, from the *More to Life DVD*; 2—My Story, the believer; 3—Your Story, your lost friend; 4—His Story, Jesus

SUMMARY AND PRAYER
(5 minutes)

No one knows how well people understand the gospel better than God. He is passionate for lost people, and He wants to use us to reach them. But to do so, we must become keenly aware of who they are and how well they understand the life of Christ.

Prayer Time
Close by praying with each other that God will give us all the confidence and desire to take the opportunities that are before us and have the thrill of seeing lives transformed—and being transformed ourselves!

One or more persons should pray aloud that Jesus' passion regarding "far from God" people will become our passion as well. Also pray for one another, that God will help us to share our stories with lost people and help them to come to a better understanding of God because they have met each one of us.

Prayer Emphasis
Lord, help me see the lost as You do and to seize opportunities with them.

Video sessions are available for download at *www.lifeway.com/downloads*.

Personal Engagement

Personal activities you can do throughout the week that will help you to remain focused on the lessons and discussions from the session.

BIBLE ENCOUNTER

Acts 1:8 says, "You will receive power when the Holy Spirit has come on you, and you will be My witnesses in Jerusalem, in all Judea and Samaria, and to the ends of the earth." The early church leaders show how the message of Jesus could be effectively communicated in various cultural settings. As the gospel was taken farther from Jerusalem, the people that heard it were increasingly less familiar with the truth.

Read Acts 2:1-47; 11:19-26; and 17:16-34 and complete the chart below:

Use this chart to list the city where the disciples ministered, the audience to whom they ministered, and how well the people understood and responded to the message of Jesus.

Text	City	Audience	Response
Acts 2:5			
Acts 11:19-21			
Acts 17:16-17			

- How did the early Christians adapt their methods to ensure that the people they were talking with understood the relevance of what they were saying?

- How can we adapt the way we minister and talk about the gospel personally to ensure that we do so in a relevant manner?

- Describe some of Paul's activities with different people in Acts 17.

- How can your story help people discover that Jesus is relevant?

REFLECTION

A church planter in Orlando said:

> "When people stop reading the Bible, all they have left to
> read is our lives."

- As people "read" your life, in what ways will they discover the truth
  about Jesus?

Use the space below to list the things that you can thank God for
because you know He is changing you and Christ can be seen in you.

Use this space to list those things that you still want to be changed,
those parts of you that mean Christ remains hidden.

As you reflect on these things, ask God to ignite a passion in your
heart that will cause you to be so grateful to Him for what He has
done in your life that you will want to share it with others.

STEPPING OUT

God's passion for the lost becomes our passion as we engage with them as real people and begin to love them as God loves them.

At a *More to Life* event, a lady who was attending said:
> "If we love people in practical and real ways then they will probably ask why we do it. In my experience talking about Jesus with people is so much easier when they know that we love them."

During this week be prepared to engage with a person that you have identified as one that you could reach. How could you express practical love toward the people around you?

Once you have had an opportunity to begin this, use the space below to describe the experience.

PRAYER

Look at the list of people that you have included in your "World of Opportunity" circle on page 18.

Pray for the following:
- For God to make Himself know to each person listed
- For you to have the confidence and desire to engage with them

As you have prayed for these people you should expect that God will help you to see and take the opportunities that will open up.

> "Honor the Messiah as Lord in your hearts. Always be ready to give a defense to anyone who asks you for a reason for the hope that is in you."
> 1 PETER 3:15

Consider the statement below. If you feel able, sign and date it.

> Lord I have prayed for opportunities and believe you will help me to know when they come along. I promise, trusting in Your power, to make and take opportunities to tell others about You— the hope that I have in You.

Name:_____

Date:_____

BUILDING EACH OTHER UP

As you have spent time during this week engaging in all sorts of
things that have challenged you, it may be that there are things
that you have learned or experienced that you feel it would be good
to share with the other members of the group. These may be
things that will really encourage them or things that you would like
to share because you feel you need help, advice, or encouragement.

Use the space below to make a note of these things so that you
don't forget what you wanted to share!

SESSION THREE

Engaging
and Giving Away
My Faith

"You have received free of charge; give free of charge."
MATTHEW 10:8

Giving and receiving gifts is a long-time tradition. Think about the excitement you felt when you were sure you knew what gift you would receive as a Christmas or birthday present. Perhaps you were given something different and felt terribly disappointed, or maybe you were given a better gift than you requested and were overwhelmed by it.

Perhaps we should become less excited about the receiving and more excited about the giving. Especially when it comes to faith in Jesus! In fact, we should consider that the more we receive from God, the more that we have to give away to others. As we gain understanding of our own salvation in Christ, then we can better engage the lost and share the truth of the gospel.

INTRODUCTION (5 minutes)

> Leader: Use the "Introduction" material
> to begin today's session.

In the previous sessions we have discovered that God can use every one of us to reach lost people with the good news of the gospel and cause rejoicing in heaven.

During this session we will look at the first story of the four-story approach to evangelism—the *More to Life DVD,* an outreach DVD. Whatever point a lost person is at on the Graspometer, watching the outreach DVD may help them begin to ask questions about faith and move farther up to the place where they want to find out more about Jesus.

OPENING SHARE TIME
(5 minutes)

> Leader: Lead participants through a review of last week's session and Personal Engagement.

Take a few minutes to share what you recorded in your "Building Each Other Up" space.

- Did you identify any specific actions you need to take?

- What effect did the biblical passages have on your passions?

- What was the most significant lesson you learned last week?

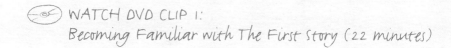 WATCH DVD CLIP 1:
    Becoming Familiar with The First Story (22 minutes)

Special Leader Note: The outreach DVD that is used in the United States is included on this DVD. If you are using a different outreach DVD, please show that version in full at this time.

> Leader: Guide participants through the following questions.

GROUP DISCUSSION *(5 minutes)*
Break into small groups of two to four people and discuss the following:

- Which stories on the DVD did you find interesting?

- Why did those particular stories stand out for you among the others?

Following the discussion, ask each of the smaller groups to share what they learned about each other with the larger group.

- How might the *More to Life DVD* connect with your current friends, neighbors, or people in your community?

Share with the group some things you learned about how people connect with the spiritual stories shared on the outreach DVD.

> Leader: Guide participants to complete the activity.

ACTIVITY

Role-Play *(8 minutes)*

The following role-play has been included as a way of providing the group with the opportunity of beginning a dialogue with another person by giving away the *More to Life DVD*. This may help you to gain some confidence in beginning a conversation and talking with another person.

Remember that the person is more likely to receive the outreach DVD if they know that you care about them and if they have seen something of Jesus in your life.

This role-play can be fun—getting things wrong and laughing about it is allowed.

Divide the group into pairs.

One person is to be chosen as the Christian offering the DVD and the other to be the person who is being offered the DVD.

Allow the person giving away the DVD to choose who it is they are giving it to. It may be most helpful if this person is from their "World of Opportunity" circle. The receiver should seek to be that person and ask questions that occur to him or her as the discussion opens up. They should not seek to be difficult!

The following opening lines may be helpful:

Giver:

"You know that I go to church. Well we're doing this special project that is aimed at sharing what we believe with people outside our church. We've got this DVD and I wondered whether you'd like to have a look at it. It's only 20 minutes long."

Receiver:

"What's on it?"

Giver:

"It has lots of stories about all different kinds of people who have become Christians. It's really interesting ..."

After the discussion has finished, repeat the role-play exercise by swapping roles.

When the role-plays are finished, discuss among the large group your observations about the ease you felt in the scenario.

GROUP DISCUSSION (5 minutes)

- From the perspective of the person receiving the outreach DVD, in what ways, if any, could the person giving the DVD have made you more willing to receive it and watch it?

- From the perspective of the Christian trying to give it away, how did it feel? What did you feel you did well? With what did you struggle?

Consider the following:

As those at the session have found each of the stories interesting for different reasons, so will some of the people that receive the outreach DVD.

It is not likely that the person who receives the outreach DVD will ask immediately "How can I become a Christian?"

It is more likely that they will ask the person who gave them the outreach DVD a question like: "Are you religious like the people on the DVD?" Answering a question like this naturally leads on to the second story—my story, which we will learn about in the next session.

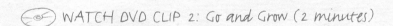 WATCH DVD CLIP 2: Go and Grow (2 minutes)

- Dennis tells the story of changing the exercise for his triceps. What do you feel needs to be changed in order to become more effective as a witness?

A common saying is:
"If you always do what you've always done then you'll always get what you've always got."

- Discuss some of the common approaches to evangelism in our church or churches in our area. How well are these approaches working?

Using the outreach DVD to begin a conversation about Jesus may be different from what many expect in doing "evangelism."

- How do you feel this different approach will help you to gain the passion and confidence to be more effective in sharing your faith?

Another possible difference is that you are often left to do evangelism on your own.

- How are you feeling about being part of this group and sharing with, praying with, and encouraging one another?

- What are some specific needs that you could share with the group to help you with personal evangelism and building witnessing relationships?

SUMMARY AND PRAYER
(5 minutes)

God wants to use each believer to reach others with the good news of Jesus. As each person has shared a little of their story and is now considering to whom they might give the outreach DVD, go back to your role-playing partner and give one another prayer requests regarding witnessing opportunities. It is important to be honest and specific about how you feel about giving away the DVD and sharing your faith with a lost person.

Prayer Time
Show support to one another by praying for these specific needs. By doing so, this group can become a place where we are increasingly honest about our needs and joys regarding our evangelistic opportunities. Remember the words of Jesus in Matthew 18:20:

> "Where two or three are gathered together in My name,
> I am there among them."

Prayer Emphasis
Lord, help me engage with the lost all around me.

As you pray for one another's strength in witnessing, be sure to also pray for the lost people you know as well.

Video sessions are available for download at *www.lifeway.com/downloads*.

Personal Engagement

Personal activities you can do throughout the week that will help you to remain focused on the lessons and discussions from the session.

BIBLE ENCOUNTER

Read Luke 10.

This chapter records the story of the followers of Jesus who had been sent out to proclaim the kingdom of God (see Luke 9:60).

Preparing to Go

Answer the following questions about the harvest fields in Luke 10:1-3.

- Jesus said the harvest is plentiful. How is this still true today?

- How did Jesus anticipate the prayer in verse 2 being answered?

- Why do you think Jesus used the image of sheep and wolves?

- What opposition do you feel you will face as you begin to share your faith with others?

- Why do you think Jesus told His disciples to take nothing with them?

- Do you trust God to do in and through you things that you cannot do alone?

Reflecting on the Experience

Read Luke 10:17-20 again regarding the return of the 72.

- Why were the 72 so thrilled?

- What did Jesus remind them was the whole purpose of following Him?

This is about a radical understanding of evangelism. We are not called to only invite people to come to our safe, well-resourced territory, otherwise known as our churches. Rather, we must leave the safety of what is familiar and go into places where we may not be welcome. We must trust in God to do through us what we cannot do alone.

REFLECTION

In Matthew 28:18-20, Jesus says:

> "All authority has been given to Me in heaven and on earth.
> Go, therefore, and make disciples of all nations, baptizing
> them in the name of the Father and of the Son and of the
> Holy Spirit, teaching them to observe everything I have
> commanded you. And remember, I am with you always,
> to the end of the age."

Use the space below to write about an occasion in your life when
you have really known that God is with you. Write about what
happened, how it felt, and in what ways it helped you to trust God
more deeply.

STEPPING OUT

You have identified people to whom you feel God is prompting you to
reach out. These names are written in your "World of Opportunity"
circle on page 18. Now is the time to begin to engage with these
people at a deeper level.

This week, give a *More to Life DVD* to at least one of the three
people in the circle. Record the event below.

PRAYER

Use the space below to write down all the things that prevent you from engaging with this person at a deeper level. List everything, not leaving anything out.

Once the list is complete, pray through it asking God to give you the confidence in Him and the desire for the lost to overcome these obstacles. Then, having prayed, trust Him!

BUILDING EACH OTHER UP

As you have spent time during this week engaging in all sorts of things that have challenged you, it may be that there are things that you have learned or experienced that you feel it would be good to share with the other members of the group. These may be things that will really encourage them or things that you would like to share because you feel you need help, advice, or encouragement.

Use the space below to make a note of these things so that you don't forget what you wanted to share!

SESSION FOUR

Talking About
My Own Story

> "Honor the Messiah as Lord in your hearts. Always be
> ready to give a defense to anyone who asks you for a
> reason for the hope that is in you."
> 1 PETER 3:15

Your story is interesting!

Some people do not believe that statement. Many Christians are especially guilty of believing they have a boring life when the truth is that a life saved by the power of God is the most interesting story of all. No matter the background—whether from a religious family or a life of crime—a person saved by God's grace has a profound story to share, and it will be interesting to all sorts of people.

We do not need to over-dramatize our spiritual story. Nor should we diminish it because we were not hardened criminals prior to our faith in Christ. Rather, we simply tell how amazing it is to have Christ working in our life every day.

INTRODUCTION (5 minutes)

Leader: Use the "Introduction"
material to begin today's session.

In the previous sessions we have discovered that God can use every one of us to reach lost people with the good news of the gospel and cause rejoicing in heaven. In this session we will look at the second story of the four-story approach to evangelism—talking about my own story.

Telling our story to a lost person who is some way down the Graspometer may help them to see the reality of God in our lives and encourage them to want to discover more about Jesus, to climb up the Graspometer.

OPENING SHARE TIME
(10 minutes)

> Leader: Lead participants through a review of last week's session and Personal Engagement.

Take a few minutes to share what you recorded in your "Building Each Other Up" space.

- Did you identify any specific actions you need to take?

- What effect did the biblical passages have on your passions?

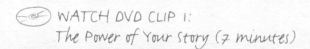 WATCH DVD CLIP 1:
The Power of Your Story (7 minutes)

> Leader: Guide participants through the following questions.

Your story is powerful because it can encourage people who know little about Jesus to become interested in finding out more.

What normally comes to our minds when you think about an "exciting" Christian testimony? Things that are familiar to you may be totally new to the person that you are speaking with and can help them to gain a much better understanding of God than they would have had if they had never met you.

- How do "dramatic" stories of redemption (deliverance from addictions, serving time in prison, etc.) help in gaining the attention of lost people?

- How can the story of an ordinary person's salvation also bring about curiosity in an unbeliever?

There are many things about your relationship with Jesus that may be of interest to a person who is beginning to discover the truth about Jesus.

Leader: Guide participants to complete the activity and discussion.

ACTIVITY
Role-Play (10 minutes)

This role-play has been included to provide the group a chance to talk about the difference that faith in Jesus is making in their lives and will help the group become more confident in sharing their stories with unbelievers.

Divide the group into pairs.

One person is to play the role of the believer who will share at least one aspect of their life that has been changing as a result of their faith in Jesus. Remember to focus on a current aspect of your life that is affected by your relationship with Christ. Our story should begin not with "what has happened" but with "what is happening" in our lives as a result of our faith in Christ.

The other person should ask questions related to what has been shared. (As in the previous role-play, they should not seek to be difficult!)

Note that the change does not have to be about dramatic things. It is more likely to be effective if it is about things that most other people face or have questions about.

Some examples of change:
- Discovering purpose or meaning in life
- The difference faith makes in how we face challenges
- Answers to prayer
- How the believer feels about themselves as a result of knowing God is in their lives
- Lifestyle changes that have taken place

When the discussion wraps up, swap roles and repeat the exercise.

GROUP DISCUSSION (10 minutes)

When the role-plays are finished, ask the group to give feedback about the experience. Specifically ask them to discuss the following:

- How did it feel to talk about personal and spiritual subjects?

- What interesting things did people hear?

Leader: Use a poster board or white board to note the answers from the group.

Dennis said that the people around us "are so busy living that they never stop to think about life."

- What are the common distractions the lost people around you deal with that are necessary to overcome in order to share your story of faith?

- In what ways does the telling of our stories help people to move farther up the Graspometer?

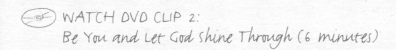

WATCH DVD CLIP 2:
   Be You and Let God Shine Through (6 minutes)

Leader: Guide participants through
the following questions.

- In the past, what have been the ways you have been taught
  to share the gospel? How have these ways been effective or
  challenging for you to use?

- Dennis described it on the video as simply telling your story in
  one-on-one conversations. How is this different from the other
  ways you have learned or thought about sharing the message
  of Jesus?

- Beginning our story with "what is happening" because of our
  faith in Christ instead of "what has happened" may impact
  a lost person's receptiveness to our story. How might this
  simple change make a difference in how we witness?

In John 9, Jesus encounters and heals a blind beggar. The beggar's
response in verse 25 when questioned about who healed him was:
   "Whether or not He's a sinner, I don't know. One thing I do
   know: I was blind, and now I can see!"

Ask for a few participants to describe the difference that Jesus is
currently making in their lives. Use the formula of the beggar below:

I was (blind) _____.

Now I (can see) _____.

Ask someone in the group to read 1 Corinthians 2:1-5 aloud:

"When I came to you, brothers, announcing the testimony of God to you, I did not come with brilliance of speech or wisdom. For I didn't think it was a good idea to know anything among you except Jesus Christ and Him crucified. I came to you in weakness, in fear, and in much trembling. My speech and my proclamation were not with persuasive words of wisdom but with a powerful demonstration by the Spirit, so that your faith might not be based on men's wisdom but on God's power"

Paul did not rely on brilliant words. Instead he simply spoke about the crucifixion of Christ and what he had come to know by his own experience of faith.

- How should this help to shape how we are speaking about spiritual truth and our own relationship with Christ?

- Imagined how different things might be if all of us were talking openly and naturally about the difference God is making in our lives—not trying to convert people instantly but helping them to have a better understanding of God than they would have had if they had never met me. What kind of difference would this change make?

In Acts 4:20, Peter and John were arrested for talking about Jesus. When ordered to stop, they said:
"We are unable to stop speaking about what we have seen and heard."

- What are the things which intimidate you into not talking about God's work in your life?

- What help do you need so that you will gain the confidence and desire to tell your story?

SUMMARY AND PRAYER
(5 minutes)

Many of us are far more aware of what we can't do than of what God can do through us. Prayer can change this!

Prayer Time
Use the remainder of the time in this session for prayer. This may be in pairs, small groups, or open prayer in a large group.

Encourage the group to pray for one another that God will equip, help, and use each one as they share their faith with people that become interested. Be specific and honest as you pray.

Prayer Emphasis
Lord, help me work with You instead of for You.

Video sessions are available for download at *www.lifeway.com/downloads*.

Personal Engagement

Personal activities you can do throughout the week that will help you to remain focused on the lessons and discussions from the session.

BIBLE ENCOUNTER
Read the Scripture passages below and answer the questions that follow.

"Whether or not He's a sinner, I don't know. One thing I do know: I was blind, and now I can see!"
JOHN 9:25

- How might you explain the difference Jesus is making in your life in one sentence?

- The man born blind knew little about Jesus but shared what he knew. What could you share with others?

"We are unable to stop speaking about what we have seen and heard."
ACTS 4:20

- What led Peter and John to make this statement?

- How is this statement true in your life?

REFLECTION

If Peter were to tell his story about his life up until this point it might go something like this:

Hi, my name is Peter. I used to be called Cephas but then I met the most remarkable Person—Jesus. I was a fisherman at the time and He told me to leave my work and everything else to follow Him. From now, He said, I would fish for men and I would be called Peter.

For about three years, I followed Him all around. There were 11 others who were really close to Him and count-less others who regularly turned up to see Him do the most remarkable things to and through us. But I guess you know most of that.

For me, following Jesus has been, more than anything, about trusting that what He said was true. I mean, I've always been ready for a challenge but I just blew it so many times.

I walked on water. Not many people have done that. After just a few seconds though, I doubted Him and started to sink. But, He rescued me.

I recognized Him for who He was, the Messiah, and then, straight away I told Him what I thought about His words. He said He was going to die and then be raised from the dead. I said, "Never." Can you believe it? How could I have been so close to the truth one minute and so far away the next?

When He was taken away to be crucified, I was afraid and denied that I ever knew Him. He said I would but I said it again, "Never." I would never disown Him, even if I had to die with Him. But I did, just like He said.

And then, after He came back from the dead, He kept asking me if I loved Him. I said yes and really meant it.

I know that He was God. And I know that He died and rose again for our sins. But I don't just know it in my head—I know it deep in here, in my heart. He has changed my life forever.

I guess the most important thing I have learned is, "Never say 'never.' " Though I doubted Him and denied knowing Him, Jesus never gave up on me. With God nothing is impossible!

There's loads of other stuff I haven't got time to mention, and you might get bored if I speak for too long. So let me finish like this.

I know something. I know that I believe in Him and what I think makes it impossible for me to stop speaking about Him. I know because He spoke the truth, because He is the truth. I know because of all the times I've blown it and He's picked me up and put me back on track.

I know that He loves me! So I can't help it—I have to tell you about Him.

- How would you tell the story of what it means to be a follower of Jesus?

Use the space below to write down some of the things that are most important in your story—since you became a Christian!

STEPPING OUT

Remember that heaven rejoices when lost people come to know Jesus and God wants you to share these things with people who are far from Him but close to you. Look back over the things you have written and then think about the names of people that you wrote down previously. How could you reach each of them by telling a part of your story?

Decide to talk to one of these people openly about an aspect of your story that is relevant to them. Do it this week and then record the event below.

PRAYER

Jesus, in Matthew 5:14-16, encourages us to live in such a way that people will see our good deeds and praise God. Paul, in Philippians 2:14-15, describes how the lives we live help the truth of God to shine. Our story is the explanation of the things that people see in our lives.

You may feel that your life is not lived in such a way that people will see your good deeds and praise God. What do you need God to change in you so that your life will shine and encourage people to become curious about what enables you to live like you do? Take some time to focus on God and write down some areas of your life that you know prevent your light shining with the gospel.

Now talk to God about these in prayer and remember that Jesus said in Matthew 7:7,

"Keep asking, and it will be given to you."

Telling Your Story

In these last two sessions of Personal Engagement, it is time for you to begin constructing your story. Perhaps you have learned how to present a gospel outline in the past. If so, you can draw from those outlines to form your own personalized way to present the truths about Christ, our need to be saved from sin, and how Christ is making a difference in your life today.

This week, focus on your story as it stands right now. Use the following questions to build a story of how God is changing your life.

- How does God help me in making decisions?
- What role does the Bible play in guiding my life?
- What is a recent example in your life of how God helped you through the midst of a difficult circumstance?
- When life is going well, how do you involve God in your everyday routine?

You do not have to answer every one of these questions. In fact, there might be other issues you wish to address in telling your story to a lost friend. Use the space on the following page to write down your story in either paragraph form or in short bullet points.

BUILDING EACH OTHER UP

As you have spent time during this week engaging in all sorts of things that have challenged you, it may be that there are things that you have learned or experienced that you feel it would be good to share with the other members of the group. These may be things that will really encourage them or things that you would like to share because you feel you need help, advice, or encouragement.

Use the space below to make a note of these things so that you don't forget what you wanted to share!

My Story

How to Hear Their Story

"The one who gives an answer before he listens—
this is foolishness and disgrace for him."
PROVERBS 18:13

This verse sounds tough, but it is filled with important meaning when we share our faith. If we do not listen to and come to know the person that we are sharing with, then our words are often unrelated to their understanding of God and mean little to them.

What was the last story someone told you today? Can you remember the details? The emotions of the person telling the story? The art of dialogue seems to have withered. We send short electronic notes to one another through e-mail, text messages, and the like. As believers, we need to show a greater interest in the thoughts of others.

The people around us are hoping that we will engage in their story, their journey. As we seek to tell the story of Christ and His salvation, we need to know how it will intersect with their lives before we can fully know how to share the gospel. We must address how we can move from just hearing to truly listening to people.

INTRODUCTION *(5 minutes)*

Leader: Use the "Introduction" material
to begin today's session.

In the previous session, we discussed the subject of telling our own story. Today, we will focus on how to become a better listener to the stories of others.

One of the great challenges in witnessing is listening to a person who does not know the truth—they don't know Jesus. Yet, to build a friendship with them, we need to value what they have to say.

Listening to the story and hearing about the life and beliefs of a lost person who is some way down the Graspometer will enable you to share aspects of your story that may help them see the reality of God in your life.

Telling your story *and* listening to theirs may become an ongoing dialogue that takes place over weeks, months, or even years. This dialogue is key in helping the lost person to want to discover more, to move up the Graspometer.

You may also find that as you engage in dialogue that your passion for this person to come to know Jesus grows deeper and deeper. As you hear about their life and get to know them they cease to be just a lost person but a person with a name and a life, a person who God loves and sent Jesus to die for. God's passion for this person begins to become real in you. As they climb the Graspometer, your passion is going deeper on the Passionometer.

OPENING SHARE TIME
(5 minutes)

Leader: Lead participants through a review of last week's session and Personal Engagement.

Take a few minutes to share what you recorded in your "Building Each Other Up" space.

- Did you identify any specific actions you need to take?

- What effect did the biblical passages have on your passions?

- Can anyone tell of an instance this week when you engaged a friend in a conversation about spiritual things? If so, share what happened.

WATCH DVD CLIP 1: Time to Listen (7 minutes)

Leader: Guide participants to interact through the following questions.

GROUP DISCUSSION (10 minutes)

- What beliefs seem to be most common among the people that are close to you?

- What are some of your fears about a having a conversation about faith with an unbeliever?

- How can conversation play a vital role in leading someone to place their faith in Christ?

- When thinking about your closest friends who are not believers, where would you place them on the Graspometer? What role will conversation potentially have in leading these friends to become Christians?

- By listening, we can begin relating parts of our own story to the story of others. What are the parts of your spiritual journey and faith in Christ that will relate to the people you listed in your "World of Opportunity" circle on page 18?

Leader: Guide participants to complete the following activity and questions.

ACTIVITY
Listening and the Graspometer
(8 minutes)

	G R A S P O M E T E R		
0	Full grasp of the Christian faith	Most evangelistic activity	Churched
-1			
-2			
-3			
-4		People becoming increasingly lost. This is where witness must be increased.	
-5	Belief in God but not committed		Less churched
-6			
-7			
-8			
-9			
-10	No idea that God exists	Often totally unreached	Never churched

As you look again at the Graspometer, ask someone in the group to read the following paragraph out loud:

> We can feel afraid of entering into a conversation because we fear that we may not know what to say in answer to questions that may come up. As evangelism is "leaving the person I have met with a better understanding of God than

they would have had if they had not met me," we can relax a little. We do not need to pretend to know what we don't know. God wants to use you as you are to help others to discover more about Jesus. Getting to know the person you are talking with is vitally important to being able to answer their questions about Jesus and faith.

- How do you feel about the previous comments?

- In what ways will listening to a person make it possible for you to help them gain a better understanding of God?

- Think about Jesus' ministry and times in which He spoke with someone and took into account their story. Look at the examples provided below to help you get started. What other examples can you add to the list?
  Martha (see Luke 10:38-42)
  Nicodemus (see John 3:1-21)
  The Samaritan woman at the well (see John 4:1-26)

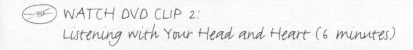 WATCH DVD CLIP 2:
Listening with Your Head and Heart (6 minutes)

Leader: Guide participants to interact through the following activity and questions.

ACTIVITY
Hearing or Listening (8 minutes)

Ask the group to break into pairs. Each person should talk about one or a couple of things that they find interesting. Take about three minutes each. It does not have to be a spiritual topic. The activity is not really about the person that is talking—it is about the one who is listening.

As you hear what the person is saying, ask questions and find out more. Try to ask open-ended questions rather than questions which can be answered with yes or no. Seek to develop the skill not just of hearing what the person says but listening to what they are saying!

GROUP DISCUSSION *(5 minutes)*

- How did you feel as you were listening and asking questions? Relaxed, the need to interject your own story, interested, bored, or something else?

- In what ways was it helpful or challenging?

- What would help you to become a better listener?

- Are there times you wish the unbelievers in your life would just "be quiet" and listen to you? How might you begin to adjust this attitude to become a better listener?

- What does being a better listener gain us in relating to unbelievers?

Ask for two or three participants to discuss the journey it took for them to come to faith. Specifically ask them to talk about the people who talked with them about the life of Jesus and took time to listen to their questions.

> Leader: Conclude the session with
> the following emphasis on prayer.

SUMMARY AND PRAYER
(5 minutes)

Unbelievers need to see that our lives match up with our dialogue in relation to the importance of Christ in our lives. Often the first step is by listening carefully to them.

By looking at Jesus' life, we see that He was a great listener. Whether listening to the stories of peoples' needs or their responses to His questions, Christ engaged normal people in conversations. He also left us an example of how to move from the dialogue to presenting the truth of who He is. Today, let's pray about how God can shape us so we can be like Jesus and engage the people around us to hear their story and tell them His story.

Use the remainder of the time in this session for prayer. This may be in pairs, small groups, or open prayer in a large group.

Prayer Time
Encourage the group to pray for one another, that God will help each person to become good listeners as well as good speakers. Also pray that God will use each person to help those being reached to gain a greater grasp of who Jesus is through them and that each person will gain a greater God-given compassion as they come to know the person or people they are listening to on a deeper level.

Prayer Emphasis
Lord, give me a discerning heart to speak like Jesus.

Video sessions are available for download at *www.lifeway.com/downloads*.

Personal Engagement

Personal activities you can do throughout the week that will help you to remain focused on the lessons and discussions from the session.

BIBLE ENCOUNTER
Read John 4:1-26 and answer the following questions.

- What are the insights that Jesus has into the life of the woman He meets?

- In what ways does Jesus use His insights to relate the truth about Himself?

- How might the insights you gain into the lives of those you come to know enable you to help them to discover more about Jesus?

REFLECTION

There is a world of difference between hearing and listening. We hear so many things and then let them pass by without processing them and, when appropriate, responding.

Consider the last week or so. In the space below, make a list of things that you have heard. Then, from that list, select the things that you really listened to and engaged in.

- Why did you engage with these? What difference did it make when you did?

STEPPING OUT

There is a real comfort in only ever talking about our faith with people at church who largely agree with what we believe. It can feel daunting to discuss faith with people who don't agree with us. However, you are engaged in *More to Life* because you want to reach your friends who do not know Christ. Remember these verses from 1 John 4:4-6 as a reminder of the victory we have in Christ:

> "You are from God, little children, and you have conquered them, because the One who is in you is greater than the one who is in the world. They are from the world. Therefore what they say is from the world, and the world listens to them. We are from God. Anyone who knows God listens to us; anyone who is not from God does not listen to us. From this we know the Spirit of truth and the spirit of deception."

This week be sure to open up a conversation with a person who is not a Christian and listen to what they have to say. Take time to reflect upon the role-playing you have done in the group sessions and prepare yourself for a spiritual conversation with a lost person. Remember that listening may be the most important thing you can do right now.

If you are a person who finds it difficult to engage in a conversation with a lost person then why not make contact with a person in your *More to Life: Engaging Through Story* group who is confident and finds it easier? Ask them to pray with you and support you as you trust God and engage in a new conversation this week.

If you are one who finds it easy to share about your relationship with Christ, then seek out those in your group you know are struggling. Ask them how you can be of help to them. Offer to pray for them or even take the person with you when you know you might share the gospel in the near future.

Write the name of the person you intend to engage in conversation with this week: _____

PRAYER

Use the conversations you have had recently as the launching point for prayer today. Take a little time to write down topics of the conversations you had with lost people over the last week and begin praying for each person by name and circumstance. For example, you may have had a discussion about children with an unbelieving neighbor. Pray for God to convict the person about their need for His help in raising their kids and how He might use you to share how your relationship with Christ makes a difference in your parenting. Use the space provided to write down names and topics.

Name   Topic

Writing Your Gospel Presentation

More to Life wants you to assemble your own gospel presentation. Often, evangelistic training comes with a prescribed presentation that you are to make to everyone you meet. However, we are learning that when we listen to a lost friend, we have the chance to learn what they need to hear about Jesus and His good news.

Below is a list of verses that are often used about God's holiness, man's sinfulness, the death and resurrection of Christ, and our need to respond with faith to His grace. Read through the verses in your Bible (even if you know them already). As you read, begin assembling your own customized gospel presentation in the space provided.

Romans 3:23
Romans 6:23
John 3:3
John 14:6
Romans 10:9-10
2 Corinthians 5:15
Revelation 3:20
Joshua 1:5
John 16:7-8
Acts 2:38
1 John 4:4
John 8:23-24
Romans 10:17
1 John 1:7
John 4:35
Ephesians 1:7
Galatians 3:11

2 Corinthians 5:21
Matthew 26:28
Mark 1:15
Acts 5:31
Romans 3:25-26
John 6:68-69
Romans 8:1-2
John 11:25-26
Joshua 1:9
2 Peter 3:9
Ephesians 2:4-5
John 3:16
Ephesians 2:8
John 14:3
Matthew 4:19
John 9:25

My Gospel Presentation

By becoming familiar with a large number of verses dealing with God, our sin, and His salvation, you will become confident in how to present the gospel to multiple people in multiple forms while sharing an unchanging message.

Begin building a presentation of the gospel that feels natural to you and flows easily from your own story of faith in Christ. Do not feel an immense amount of pressure to finish it in one setting. Work on it over several days. In next week's Personal Engagement section, you will be asked to bring it to completion.

BUILDING EACH OTHER UP

As you have spent time during this week engaging in all sorts of things that have challenged you, it may be that there are things that you have learned or experienced that you feel it would be good to share with the other members of the group. These may be things that will really encourage them or things that you would like to share because you feel you need help, advice, or encouragement.

Use the space below to make a note of these things so that you don't forget what you wanted to share!

SESSION SIX
Telling His Story

"I am not ashamed of the gospel, because it is God's power for salvation to everyone who believes."
ROMANS 1:16

After several weeks of training, hopefully you are ready to get going with something new in your life. Perhaps you have already become more active in conversing about your faith. If that is the case—keep up the good work!. If not, make yourself available by closely watching your relationships. Most likely, God intends to provide new opportunities for you to build witnessing relationships.

INTRODUCTION (5 minutes)

> Leader: Use the "Introduction" material to begin today's session.

Special Leader Note: For this session, create an atmosphere similar to what you would expect for a *Discover More to Life* group: casual gathering with friends such as a living room, coffee shop, or other inviting location. This session will be a sample of session one of *Discover More to Life*. It is important that those in *More to Life: Engaging Through Story* get a positive feel for what the *Discover More to Life* gatherings will be like.

This closing section is about the fourth story, the most exciting and meaningful story of all—the story of Jesus!

Beginning a conversation with the first story and the outreach DVD then engaging in a dialogue of telling your story and listening to the story of an unbeliever may, over a period of time, help that person climb up the Graspometer to the point where they are now really wanting to find out more about Jesus.

People who were -10 or even -5 on the Graspometer when we first gave them the outreach DVD are unlikely, even now, to want to attend church or a Bible-study group. They may now be around -3 and wanting to know the truth about Jesus. If they are to hear and understand the gospel then we can communicate it to them in one of two ways:

1. We can share the gospel with them.
2. We can invite them to an informal group where they can discover faith in Jesus. These groups are called *Discover More to Life*.

OPENING SHARE TIME *(5 minutes)*

Leader: Lead participants through a review of last week's lesson and Personal Engagement.

Take a few minutes and share a key lesson you learned from last week's Personal Engagement work.

• Did you identify any specific actions you need to take?

• What effect did the biblical passages have on your passions?

• Did you have any encounters with lost people this week in which you were able to share part of your story or hear part of their story? If so, tell what happened.

WATCH DVD CLIP 1: *Sharing the Gospel (7 minutes)*

Leader: Guide participants through the
following questions and activity.

GROUP DISCUSSION *(5 minutes)*

- What has been your normal reaction to the opportunity
  to share the gospel with a lost person? Excitement,
  nervousness, or hesitancy? What might explain your feelings?

ACTIVITY
Role-Play (8 minutes)

During the personal engagement time since we last met, we have
had the opportunity to write our own gospel presentation. Break
into pairs and take a few minutes to share the gospel using what
you have written.

One person is to play the role of the believer who will share their
own gospel presentation. (Remember to focus on a current
aspect of your life that is affected by your relationship with
Christ!) As you share, consider what stories you may use to
help the listener understand the truth that you are seeking to
communicate.

The other person should ask questions related to what has been
shared. (Again, they should not seek to be difficult!)

After the discussion ends, repeat the exercise by swapping roles.

 WATCH DVD CLIP 2:
   An Introduction to Discover More to Life (5 minutes)

AN INTRODUCTION TO DISCOVER MORE TO LIFE
(8 minutes)

Take some time to discuss the following:

- How do you feel that Jesus is relevant to people who are searching for love, purpose, and meaning in life?

Dennis underlined the importance of inviting the person you have been sharing with to come with you to *Discover More to Life*.

- In pairs share ways that you will be inviting or plan to invite others to *Discover More to Life*. Be encouraging and help each other to gain the confidence to make the invitation!

 WATCH DVD CLIP 3: *The Cascade Effect* (4 minutes)

GROUP DISCUSSION *(5 minutes)*

Your study of *More to Life: Engaging Through Story* may appear to be over. But remember what Dennis said: "It starts now!"

- What steps does God want you to take?

- Describe a few ways you have been encouraged through the process of participating in this training group.

- How might you respond to the four challenges Dennis gave at the end of the video today?

1. Use the *More to Life DVD*.
   I will use the outreach DVD to engage with lost people who are far from God and close to me.

Who is the first person you would like to give an outreach DVD?

2. Lead a *More to Life: Engaging Through Story* group.
   I will invite some Christian friends and complete a More to Life: Engaging Through Story *group with them.*

Who are three friends in the church you would like to invite to a *More to Life: Engaging Through Story* group?

3. Host a *Discover More to Life* group.
   I will host and facilitate a Discover More to Life *group.*

Over the last month, who are you most passionate about involving into a *Discover More to Life* group?

4. Become an advocate for *More to Life*.
   I will become an advocate for More to Life *and encourage others to become part of what God is doing through this ministry.*

How can you help spread your excitement about the *More to Life* approach to evangelism?

As a final exercise, read the following statement and answer the accompanying questions:

"Imagine a day when people are lining up to get out of church in order to take the gospel to our community."

- How would that change our community?

- How would it change our church?

- How would it change you?

SUMMARY AND PRAYER
(5 minutes)

Use the remainder of the time in this session for prayer. This may be in pairs, small groups, or open prayer in a large group.

This is the final session of the study, and those who have taken part will have experienced many things. They may have been challenged, encouraged, or renewed. They may have engaged in great conversations and shared their success or secretly feel failure because their attempts to share have just not happened and they still feel cramped with fear and guilt.

Use this time to pray that God will be involved in the life of each person in the group and that He will help each of them to take the next step in making Him known.

Prayer Emphasis
Lord give each person what we need to step out in faith and make You known.

Video sessions are available for download at *www.lifeway.com/downloads*.

Personal Engagement

Personal activities you can do throughout the week that will help you to remain focused on the lessons and discussions from the session.

BIBLE ENCOUNTER
Read Matthew 7:24-27:

"Everyone who hears these words of Mine and acts on them will be like a sensible man who built his house on the rock. The rain fell, the rivers rose, and the winds blew and pounded that house. Yet it didn't collapse, because its foundation was on the rock. But everyone who hears these words of Mine and doesn't act on them will be like a foolish man who built his house on the sand. The rain fell, the rivers rose, the winds blew and pounded that house, and it collapsed. And its collapse was great!"

Jesus is referring to obedience in these words and is teaching that it is not enough to have heard Him speak to you. It is important that you do what you have heard Him say.

- What are some of the main things that you have "heard" Jesus say to you throughout this course?

- What are the consequences of putting into practice what you have heard? What would the house standing mean to you in relation to what Jesus has said?

- What are the consequences of not putting into practice what you have heard? What would the house falling mean to you in relation to what Jesus has said?

REFLECTION

James 1:22-25 presents the picture of a person looking in the mirror and then, as they leave, forgetting what they look like. This image is related to how we can easily make the mistake of, as James says, looking closely.

Read James 1:22-25:

"Be doers of the word and not hearers only, deceiving yourselves. Because if anyone is a hearer of the word and not a doer, he is like a man looking at his own face in a mirror. For he looks at himself, goes away, and immediately forgets what kind of man he was. But the one who looks intently into the perfect law of freedom and perseveres in it, and is not a forgetful hearer but one who does good works—this person will be blessed in what he does."

Stand in front of a mirror and on this occasion not for the purposes of vanity or personal hygiene but just so you can see yourself—a creature of God. As you stand there and can see your reflection, talk to God. Speak to Him about the things that you have learned from Him about your life and His Spirit's prompting He may have given you to talk with somebody about Him. As you begin this, you might be surprised by the way things occur to you. Say them out loud to God as you look at yourself, His child, who He wants to use to play the part God has for you in reaching the lost.

When you feel that you have said all that there is to say, make a promise to God, trusting in His help. Promise that you will put into practice those things that you have heard Him say.

There is a world of difference between hearing and listening. We hear so many things and then let them pass by without processing them and, when appropriate, responding.

Record the lessons God has taught you through this exercise.

STEPPING OUT

Moving from study to action has been a theme throughout this study. Now that you have reached the conclusion, it is time for you to commit to three key actions:

1. I will find ways to engage the unbelievers around me in spiritual conversations.
2. I will start and/or participate in a *Discover More to Life* group.
3. I will offer to lead a *More to Life: Engaging Through Story* group for my church.

Jesus wants you to make Him known. If you are willing, then as an act of commitment, sign your name agreeing to keep the promise.

Name_____ Date_____

My Gospel Story

In session five, you took the time to write down your own story. Perhaps you included details such as when you became a Christian and who led you to a proper understanding of the gospel. Hopefully, you were able to record how Jesus, and faith in Him, makes a difference in how you live life, face trials, and celebrate your blessings.

Today, take time to finish crafting your gospel presentation. Look back on the list of verses on pages 74–75 and the work you began in crafting a customized gospel presentation.

PRAYER

Take a moment and read the following prayer:

Lord Jesus, I thank You that You acted in obedience to the Father and came to this world to seek and to save the lost. I know it cost You an extraordinary amount. Thank You that because of all You went through, now I can know God.

Now Lord, I know that You are sending me to play my part in telling Your story. I know there may be a cost, but I will go. Thank You that as I make this promise to You, I know You will keep Your promise to go with me.

I will go.

As you pray today, make this type of commitment to God that you will be a person who is constantly "going" to the unbelievers who are around you.

BUILDING EACH OTHER UP

In the Stepping Out section of our Personal Engagement, you had the opportunity to commit to leading a *More to Life: Engaging Through Story* group. Whether or not you have led Bible-study classes or training courses before, you can do it. The *More to Life: Engaging Through Story* book is designed so that once a person has attended a class, they are fully prepared to lead the training. All you have to do is simply review the material each week and use the embedded "Leader's Notes" to guide a group of participants through the study. If you have a passion for sharing about your relationship with Christ and helping other believers to do the same, then you are ready to be a leader in *More to Life: Engaging Through Story*.

Sit down with the person who led you through this training and ask them to help you in forming a new *More to Life: Engaging Through Story* group.

LEADER GUIDE

Thanks for giving your time and effort to lead a *More to Life: Engaging Through Story* group. It will be a challenge and a blessing to lead a group of people that is being encouraged to trust in God and equipped to make Jesus known.

In 1 Thessalonians 5:11, Paul writes: "Encourage one another and build each other up." These words are so important to consider because leading this group involves more than just going through the material. It involves helping each participant to discover how they can play their unique part in making Jesus known to others. Many believers lack the confidence to share their faith and need to be, as the verse says, "encourage" and "build up."

The word encourage means "fill with courage." As many believers are fearful of engaging in faith sharing, please ensure as a leader that you are encouraging. Please also aim to ensure that each member within the group both gives and receives encouragement.

"Building each other up" is the purpose of being together. So often faith sharing is a lonely and solitary thing that each believer feels they have to do alone and unsupported. Ensure that your group is one where each member is built up to become stronger because they are in this group. Honest sharing, constant affirmation, and having fun being together will help participants to be built up and become stronger.

For each group session, we recommend a meeting time of one hour and provide guidelines in the group sessions on how much time to spend in each section of material. (You may adjust these times as needed.) You will need the *More to Life: Engaging Through Story DVD*, a television, and a DVD player for each session. You may also want to supply poster board or a white board, markers, paper, and pens for participants or encourage them to bring their own. Name tags may be appropriate for the first few group sessions.

At the first group session, distribute *More to Life: Engaging Through Story* books to all participants if they do not already have them. Be sure that participants have the opportunity to get to know one another. The better participants know each other, the more likely they will feel comfortable sharing with others what they are learning and experiencing in how to better tell unbelievers about Jesus. As a leader, encourage all participants to engage in discussion questions and activities.

Group session material has been developed around the *More to Life: Engaging Through Story DVD*. During each session, your group will watch two or three different DVD teaching segments. After you watch each DVD segment, your group will complete the discussion questions and activities that follow it. (For example, after watching DVD Clip 1, the group will discuss the questions and complete the activities that follow until DVD Clip 2.)

Each group session of *More to Life: Engaging Through Story* includes Leader Notes throughout the text. These notes guide you through the session. It would be most beneficial for you to read through each session and watch the DVD teaching segments before your group meets. However, if time does not allow for that, use the Leader Notes to help you and participants as you complete each group session.

As you work through each session, you may find that time does not allow for your group to cover all of the included material. Though we have provided time guidelines to best cover all material in *More to Life: Engaging Through Story*, your group may spend more or less time than suggested on a certain topic or other things may come up that are more appropriate to discuss. That's OK! Be flexible, and trust in God and His Spirit to guide each session. The most important thing for you to do as a leader is to ensure that participants are being better equipped to share Jesus with unbelievers. That's what *More to Life: Engaging Through Story* is all about!

Each group session includes:
- Introduction—Scripture and material that introduces the session's focus.
- Opening Share Time—an opportunity to reflect on things participants learned or experienced through the previous session's Personal Engagement section.
- Activity and Group Discussion—activities and questions that will help participants become better equipped to share Jesus with unbelievers.
- Summary and Prayer—concluding summary of the session with specific prayer needs for participants to lift up to God about becoming better at reaching others for Him.

Following each group session is a section called "Personal Engagement." Personal Engagement provides group members with an opportunity to further engage the lessons and discussions from the group session. Encourage all members to complete the Personal Engagement material before your group's next session, and be sure to review what material has been covered in the Opening Share Time. Recognize that some members may not have adequate time to finish all material so encourage them to complete as much as possible. Even if they are unable to finish the Personal Engagement material, they should still be encouraged to attend the next group session.

Each Personal Engagement section includes:
- Bible Encounter—getting to grips with Scripture that is relevant to what is being discovered and experienced.
- Reflection—personalizing what is being experienced and responding to God.
- Stepping Out—practical things we can do outside of our comfort zone.
- Prayer—transparently opening ourselves up to God.
- Building Each Other Up—noting things that we are experiencing that may be good to share with others during the group discussions.

OPTIONAL SESSION SEVEN

Many things may have occurred during the past six weeks of your group's *More to Life: Engaging Through Story*. You may find it beneficial for your group to gather for an optional seventh session to recap all the things that you have learned or experienced in your journey. This gathering should be informal (not a traditional church meeting). You may meet in someone's home, serve dinner, or share coffee and pastries. Whatever your group chooses, be sure that the setting is casual so that all participants feel comfortable engaging in conversation about their experiences.

Suggested Topics for Session Seven

Your group may decide to discuss some or all of the topics listed below or focus on other things that may have come up during your *More to Life: Engaging Through Story* group. Allow the Spirit to lead your group's discussion, and encourage all participants to share as they feel comfortable. Below is a sampling (though not exhaustive!) of some topics to discuss:

- The Passionometer: How has your level on the Passionometer changed throughout *More to Life: Engaging Through Story*?
- The Graspometer: How does the Graspometer help you in sharing your faith with the unbelievers around you?
- My Story (p. 61): Share your story with a partner or the group as if telling an unbeliever. What things has God shown you that are important to include? You could also discuss the concerns you have realized as you have developed your story. What things are hindering you that the group may be able to help you with? If you have shared your story with an unbeliever, tell about the experience.
- My Gospel Presentation (p. 75): Share with a partner or the group your gospel presentation with Scripture. What verses has God led you to include? Why do you feel these verses are important for unbelievers to hear?

MORE TO LIFE
FAMILY OF RESOURCES

**More to Life:
Engaging Through Story
DVD and Member Book**
Guides believers to share their faith through the four-story approach used in the More to Life family of resources.
DVD Kit, Item 005502439
Book, Item 005502440

More to Life: Real People, Real Stories DVD
True stories of people whose lives have changed since meeting Jesus. Share this outreach DVD with unbelievers.
Item 005187917

**Discover More to Life
DVD and Member Book**
A small-group study for unbelievers interested in learning more about a personal relationship with Jesus.
DVD Kit, Item 005502438
Book, Item 005502448

To order *More to Life* resources: write to LifeWay Church Resources Customer Service; One LifeWay Plaza; Nashville, TN 37234-0113; phone toll free (800) 458-2772; fax (615) 251-5933; order online at *www.lifeway.com;* e-mail *orderentry@lifeway.com;* or visit the LifeWay Christian Store serving you.